THE DAY AFTER AGI

A Human's Guide to Life, Purpose, and Survival

When Machines Begin to Think

Anuzka
Anshuman Sharma

Aegis India PL

For everyone who has ever stared at a screen and wondered,
"Am I about to be replaced?"
You are not. But you are about to be changed. This book is about choosing how.

"We are called to be architects of the future, not its victims."
— R. Buckminster Fuller

Copyright

Cover design: Shubham

The day after AGI, First Edition

Published by Aegis India PL

Contents

Copyright....3
Contents....4
Introduction....5
What and Why of AGI....10
The Day It Arrives....18
The Great Displacement....28
The End of Not Knowing....38
The Power Question....46
The Meaning Crisis....53
The Human Advantage....62
Children of the Transition....69
The Ethics of Creating God....77
How to Prepare....85
A Letter to the Morning After....94
A Note on Sources and Stories....98
About Authors....99
Anuzka....99
Anshuman Sharma....99

Introduction

The Phone Call at 3 a.m.

On March 14, 2023, a software engineer named Kiran sat alone in his apartment in San Francisco, staring at a screen. He had just spent four hours talking to GPT-4, which OpenAI had released to the public that day. He had asked it to write code. It wrote better code than most of his colleagues. He asked it to debug a problem that had taken his team three days. It solved the problem in eleven seconds. He asked it to explain quantum entanglement to a five-year-old, then to a physics professor, then in the style of a country song. It nailed all three.

Kiran picked up the phone and called his mother in Hyderabad. It was 3 a.m. in India. She answered on the second ring, the way mothers do when their children call at strange hours.

"Mom," he said. "I think everything is about to change."

His mother, who had spent thirty years as a schoolteacher, paused. Then she asked a question that was far wiser than anything the AI had said all evening: "Change for whom, Kiran?"

'Change for whom?' and 'What does it actually mean to be a human being in a world where machines are learning to think?' are the questions this book attempts to answer,

Because something extraordinary is happening right now. Not in the future. Not in science fiction. Right now, as you hold this book, artificial intelligence systems are writing legal briefs, discovering new proteins, composing music that makes people weep, diagnosing diseases with accuracy that rivals experienced physicians, and conducting conversations so fluid and perceptive that millions of people have begun forming emotional attachments to them.

And all of this, every headline, every breakthrough, every moment of wonder and anxiety you have felt watching this unfold, is a warmup act. The main event has not yet arrived.

The main event is called Artificial General Intelligence, or AGI, a system that can match or exceed human cognitive ability across every domain. Not a tool that is brilliant at one thing and useless at everything else, like today's AI. A system that can think. That can reason across fields the way a human mind does. That can learn something new in the morning and apply it to a completely different problem by afternoon. That can, in a meaningful sense, understand.

When, not if, this happens, every assumption you hold about work, education, creativity, purpose, economic value, and what it means to be human will be tested. Some of those assumptions will survive. Many will not. The ones that survive will be the ones that were always truly, deeply, irreplaceably human. And discovering which ones those are is among the most urgent and most beautiful projects any generation has ever faced.

This book is built on a simple conviction, that ordinary people deserve honest, clear, compassionate guidance about what is coming. Not hype. Not doom. Not the kind of vague reassurance that says "don't worry, technology always creates more jobs than it destroys" without acknowledging that this time might be fundamentally different. And not the nihilistic fatalism that says "it's all over, nothing you do matters", because that is a lie, and a particularly dangerous one.

What we will offer you in these pages is something harder and more useful than optimism or pessimism, we will offer you clarity. We will tell you, as honestly as we can, what AGI is, how close it may be, what it will likely do to your work and your world, and, most importantly, what you can do, starting today, to meet it not as a victim but as a conscious, prepared, fully alive human being.

Along the way, we will introduce you to people who are already navigating this transition, a radiologist in Nigeria who watched AI match her diagnostic skill and found something deeper on the other side; a factory worker in Michigan who lost his job to automation and discovered a calling he never knew he had; a twelve-year-old in Seoul who is growing up in a world where her homework helper is smarter than her teachers; and a retired philosophy professor in Buenos Aires who believes that AGI may force humanity to answer the question it has been avoiding for three thousand years, 'What are we actually for?'

Their stories are not fairy tales. Some are painful. Some are unresolved. All are true in the ways that matter most. And together, they form a map, not a complete one, because no map of uncharted territory can be complete, but an honest one, of the landscape we are all about to enter.

Kiran's mother asked the right question. Change for whom?

The answer is for you, for future generations and for every person on Earth.

We want to be clear about one thing before we begin, we are not going to pretend that this transition will be painless. It will not. There will be disruption, confusion, and genuine loss. There will be people who are harmed by the transition before its benefits are widely shared. There will be periods when the future looks more frightening than promising.

But we are also not going to pretend that we are helpless. We are not. The human species has navigated extraordinary transitions before, from hunter-gatherer societies to agricultural civilizations, from feudalism to democracy, from analog to digital. Each transition involved genuine suffering and genuine adaptation. Each one was shaped, for better or worse, by the choices that ordinary people and their leaders made during the period of greatest uncertainty. And each one ultimately revealed new dimensions of what it means to be human that the previous era could not have imagined.

AGI will be no different, except in scale. The scale will be larger than anything that has come before. Which means the preparation must be more serious, more deliberate, and more deeply human than anything we have attempted before.

Let's understand what's coming. Let's prepare. And let's do it together.

What and Why of AGI

What AGI Actually Is and Why This Time Is Different

> *"The development of full artificial intelligence could spell the end of the human race... It would take off on its own, and redesign itself at an ever-increasing rate." — Stephen Hawking, BBC Interview, 2014*

Let us tell you about two moments that changed how the world thinks about intelligence.

The first happened in March 1997, when an IBM computer called Deep Blue defeated Garry Kasparov, the greatest chess player in human history, in a six-game match. Kasparov, who had once declared that a computer could never beat him, sat at the table in stunned silence after the decisive game. He later described the experience in terms that sound almost spiritual. He said he sensed "a new kind of intelligence" across the board from him.

The world gasped. Editorials declared the dawn of machine supremacy. The New York Times ran the headline on the front page. It felt, to many people, like the beginning of the end.

It was not. Deep Blue could do exactly one thing, play chess at a superhuman level. It could not play checkers. It could not hold a conversation. It could not recognize a photograph of its own hardware. It was the most powerful specialist ever created, and it was dumber than a toddler at everything outside its specialty.

The second moment happened twenty-six years later, in the spring of 2023, when researchers at OpenAI published the technical report for GPT-4. Buried among the performance benchmarks was an extraordinary fact, GPT-4 had passed the Uniform Bar Exam in the 90th percentile. It had scored in the 88th percentile on the LSAT. It could write software, compose poetry, analyze medical images, explain quantum mechanics, draft legal contracts, and debate philosophy, all within the same system, with no specialized training for any individual task.

This was something Deep Blue could never do. This was not a specialist. This was the first glimpse, blurry, imperfect, but unmistakable, of something general.

The difference between these two moments is the difference between a very powerful calculator and something that is starting, however crudely, to think the way we think. And understanding that difference is the first step toward understanding everything that follows in this book.

Artificial General Intelligence (AGI) is the term researchers use for a system that can perform any intellectual task that a human being can perform, across any domain, with equal or greater capability. It is not a smarter chatbot. It is not a faster search engine. It is a mind, or something so close to a mind that the distinction may stop mattering.

Here is what makes AGI different from every AI system that currently exists. Today's AI, even the most impressive, is what researchers call "narrow", it excels within specific domains and fails, sometimes spectacularly, outside them. A language model that can write a brilliant essay about Shakespeare may confidently tell you that 7 plus 8 equals 13. An image recognition system that can identify cancer cells with superhuman accuracy may fail to recognize that the image has been rotated upside down. These systems are savants, astonishingly gifted in their domains, astonishingly limited everywhere else.

AGI is not a savant. AGI is a generalist. It can transfer knowledge between domains the way you do when you notice that managing a difficult employee is a lot like training a stubborn dog, different context, same underlying principle. It can encounter a genuinely novel problem, one it has never seen and was never trained on, and reason its way to a solution. It can set its own goals, evaluate its own progress, and improve its own methods.

In short, AGI can do the thing that has made human beings the dominant species on Earth, it can think flexibly across the full range of intellectual challenges. And once a machine can do that, the game changes in ways that are genuinely without precedent in the 300,000-year history of our species.

Now, a reasonable question, 'How close are we?'

The honest answer is that nobody knows with certainty. But the range of expert estimates has narrowed dramatically in recent years, and the direction of the narrowing should get your attention. In 2020, a survey of leading AI researchers found that the median estimate for a 50 percent chance of AGI was 2060. By 2023, after the release of GPT-4 and the rapid advancement of multimodal systems, a new survey found the median had shifted to 2040. Some of the most prominent researchers in the field, people who have spent their careers building these systems, now believe it could happen within the next decade.

Dario Amodei, the CEO of Anthropic, one of the leading AI safety companies, has publicly stated that he believes powerful AI systems could arrive as soon as 2026 or 2027. Sam Altman, the CEO of OpenAI, has said that AGI is "coming sooner than most people think." Geoffrey Hinton, often called the godfather of deep learning, resigned from Google in 2023 specifically to speak freely about the risks he sees on the horizon.

These are not fringe voices. These are the people building the technology. When they say something extraordinary is approaching, it is worth paying attention.

But we want to be careful here, because honesty demands it. The history of AI is littered with premature predictions. In 1967, Marvin Minsky, one of the founders of the field, predicted that within a generation, the problem of creating artificial intelligence would be "substantially solved." It was not. The decades that followed brought what researchers call "AI winters", periods of disappointment and dried-up funding when the technology failed to live up to the hype.

So is this time different? We believe it is, for three specific reasons.

First, the **scaling laws**. Researchers have discovered that as you increase the size of AI models, more parameters, more training data, more computational power, capabilities do not merely improve. They emerge. Abilities that did not exist at one scale suddenly appear at the next, like water unexpectedly turning to steam when it hits 212 degrees. GPT-3 could write mediocre poetry. GPT-4, which is larger, can pass professional exams. Nobody programmed these capabilities in. They emerged from scale itself. And the models are still getting larger, fast.

Second, **the investment**. The amount of money flowing into AI research and infrastructure is unprecedented in the history of technology. Hundreds of billions of dollars, from governments, corporations, and sovereign wealth funds, are being poured into the race to build more capable systems. This is not speculative venture capital; this is strategic national investment on the scale of the Manhattan Project or the Apollo program.

Third, and most importantly, the **rate of improvement**. The gap between GPT-3 (released in 2020) and GPT-4 (released in 2023) was enormous. The gap between today's systems and what is being built right now in laboratories around the world may be equally enormous. We are not crawling toward AGI. We are accelerating.

Does this mean AGI will arrive next year? No. Does it mean AGI is inevitable? No. There may be fundamental barriers we have not yet encountered. The scaling laws may plateau. The engineering challenges may prove intractable. Uncertainty is real, and I will not pretend otherwise.

But here is what we know for certain, the possibility of AGI within our lifetimes is no longer science fiction. It is a serious, evidence-based probability that the most informed people on Earth are actively preparing for. And the question of what happens when it arrives, to your job, your family, your sense of purpose, your understanding of what makes you valuable, is a question that deserves your serious attention right now, regardless of the exact timeline.

Because here is the thing about transformative change. It rewards the people who prepare early and punishes the people who prepare late. The time to think about what AGI means for your life is not the day it arrives. It is today.

Action Steps

First, spend one hour this week reading about the current state of AI from a credible source—not social media commentary, but the actual reporting from outlets like MIT Technology Review, The Atlantic, or Nature. Notice what surprises you.

Second, make a list of the five most important intellectual tasks in your daily work. For each one, honestly assess: Could today's AI already do this task reasonably well? The answers may unsettle you, and that is the point.

Third, have a real conversation with someone you trust about AGI. Not about robots in movies, but about the actual technology and what it might mean for both of your lives. You will learn more from one honest conversation than from a dozen articles.

Fourth, write down the single thing you believe a machine could never do as well as a human being. Hold that belief gently. By the time you finish this book, you may revise it.

The Day It Arrives

What the First Week Will Actually Look Like

"The future is already here, it's just not evenly distributed."— William Gibson

Forget what you have seen in the movies. There will be no robot standing in a public square. No red-eyed machine declaring war on humanity. No single dramatic moment when the lights flicker and everything changes at once.

The day AGI arrives will look, for most people, like a Tuesday.

You will wake up. You will check your phone. You will make coffee. The children will need breakfast. The traffic will be approximately what it always is. And somewhere, in a computing cluster spread across three continents, in a secure laboratory in San Francisco or London or Shenzhen, a team of exhausted researchers will be sitting in a conference room, looking at a set of test results, and not speaking.

They will not be silent because they are confused. They will be silent because they understand exactly what they are looking at, and the understanding is too large to process with words.

The system they have been building has just completed a battery of evaluations designed to measure cognitive performance across every domain of human intellectual activity, scientific reasoning, creative expression, strategic planning, social understanding, ethical judgment, mathematical proof, language comprehension, and crucially, the ability to transfer insights from one domain to another, the hallmark of genuine general intelligence.

It has not merely passed. It has exceeded human expert performance in nearly every category.

One of the researchers, a woman who has spent twelve years working toward this moment, will later describe what she felt as "the opposite of surprise, like watching something you always knew was coming finally come, and realizing that knowing it was coming didn't prepare you at all."

Within hours, the company's legal team, communications team, and government relations team will be activated. Calls will be made to intelligence agencies, regulatory bodies, and heads of state. Non-disclosure agreements that were signed years ago will suddenly matter very much. A press release will be drafted, revised, revised again, and argued over word by word by people who understand that the language they choose will be read by historians for centuries.

And here is the part that matters most for you and me, 'while all of this is happening, most of the world will not know. Not yet.'

The news will leak, as all extraordinary news eventually leaks. The first reports will be fragmentary, speculative, and often wrong. Social media will explode with rumors. Cable news will bring on experts who know a great deal and pundits who know nothing, and they will be given equal airtime. There will be a period, days, maybe weeks, during which the world both knows and does not know what has happened. A fog of half-information, during which the most consequential decisions in human history will be made by a very small number of people.

This is not speculation. This is the pattern that every major technological disclosure has followed, from the atomic bomb to the mapping of the human genome to the Snowden revelations. The pattern is consistent, the technology exists before the public knows it exists, and the gap between those two moments is shaped by power, secrecy, and institutional self-interest.

Let us walk you through what the first week will probably feel like for real people.

Amara is forty-two years old, a radiologist in Lagos, Nigeria. She has spent twelve years, more than twelve thousand hours, training her eyes to read medical images with the precision of a master. She can spot a tumor that a less experienced colleague would miss. This skill is not just her livelihood, it is her identity. When she introduces herself at dinner parties, she does not say "I work in healthcare." She says "I'm a radiologist." The skill and the self are fused.

On the morning the announcement breaks, Amara's colleague knocks on her office door and says, "Have you seen the news?" By that afternoon, Amara has read the announcement three times. She has watched four hours of analysis. She has called colleagues in London and New York. And she cannot decide whether to feel threatened or excited, because both feelings are entirely justified.

She knows, without anyone needing to tell her, that a system capable of human-level performance across all cognitive domains is also capable of reading medical images at least as well as she can. She has watched narrow AI systems approach her level of skill over the past five years. This is something else entirely. And the question that keeps circling in her mind, a question she cannot yet answer, is "If a machine can do what I do, who am I?"

• • •

Marcus is nineteen, a computer science student in Berlin. He has dreamed of working in AI since he was fourteen. The announcement fills him with a feeling he cannot quite name, something between euphoria and vertigo. Because if AGI can do everything he was planning to spend his career learning to do, what is his career now? What does a young person study when the world's most powerful mind is no longer a person at all?

Li Wei is seventy-one, a retired schoolteacher in a small city in Sichuan Province, China. Her granddaughter explains the announcement over dinner, imperfectly but with the breathless passion of a twenty-year-old who has been following AI for years. Li Wei listens carefully. Then she asks a question that her granddaughter will think about for the rest of her life:

"Does it know how to be kind?"

It is not a sophisticated question. It may be the most important question anyone asks in the first week.

Meanwhile, in the financial markets, something unprecedented is happening. Within milliseconds of any credible signal that the announcement is genuine, trading algorithms will react. Volatility will spike beyond anything in modern market history, because every financial model ever built assumes that human cognition is the primary engine of economic value, and that assumption has just been shattered. Trading halts will cascade across global exchanges. The models cannot price a future they were not designed to imagine.

Governments will scramble. Intelligence agencies that have been monitoring AI development for years will shift into crisis mode, not because the announcement is entirely unexpected, but because the gap between monitoring a technology and governing it is enormous. Emergency meetings will convene in Washington, Beijing, Brussels, and New Delhi. The questions will be urgent and largely unanswerable, "Does an AGI system have legal status? Who has jurisdiction? What restrictions can be imposed, and by whom? What happens when one nation's AGI policy conflicts with another's?"

No existing international framework was built for this. The United Nations, the World Trade Organization, the various arms control treaties, all were designed for a world of nation-states managing physical technologies within geographic boundaries. AGI is not physical and not territorial. The governance architecture will need to be built from scratch, by people who are simultaneously managing the immediate fallout, under extraordinary pressure, with the whole world watching.

And ordinary people, people like you, like us, like Amara and Marcus and Li Wei, will move through the first week in a psychological state that grief researchers would recognize immediately. Because what is happening is, in a real sense, a death, the death of a set of assumptions about what human beings are for, what our intelligence means, and why we matter.

Denial will come first, and it will be widespread. We have been told before that AI was about to change everything, and it didn't. Plenty of intelligent people will argue, with genuine evidence, that this is another false alarm, another overhyped demo that will fall apart under real-world pressure. Some of that skepticism will be correct in the short term. Much of it will be motivated reasoning, the mind protecting itself from an idea that is too large and too threatening to absorb all at once.

Then anger, bargaining, confusion. Social media will be a firestorm of hot takes, conspiracy theories, and genuine anguish. Some people will demand that the technology be destroyed. Others will demand immediate access. Most will simply feel unmoored, cast adrift in a world that suddenly looks very different from the one they went to bed in.

And eventually, unevenly, imperfectly, something else will begin to emerge, the realization that the question is not whether AGI changes everything. The question is what we do with the change. Whether we meet it with fear or with courage. Whether we let it diminish us or expand us. Whether we use this moment, this extraordinary, terrifying, once-in-a-civilization moment, to finally ask and answer the questions about human purpose that we have been avoiding for millennia.

• • •

That is what this book is about. Not the technology. The humanity.

But we want to add something before we move on, because it matters. The first week after AGI will also reveal something beautiful about human beings. In every crisis in recorded history, every earthquake, every pandemic, every war, alongside the panic and the selfishness, there has always been an extraordinary outpouring of mutual aid, compassion, and solidarity. Neighbors help neighbors. Strangers help strangers. People discover reserves of generosity and courage they did not know they possessed.

This will happen after AGI too. Communities will come together. People will reach out to each other. Teachers will stay late to help students process what is happening. Parents will hold their children a little tighter and have conversations they have been putting off. Religious leaders, community organizers, therapists, and artists will step into the breach, offering meaning and connection in a moment of collective disorientation.

And here is what we find most hopeful, the very qualities that AGI cannot replicate, empathy, vulnerability, the willingness to sit with someone in confusion and say "I do not know what is happening either, but I am here", are the exact qualities that will be most needed in the first week. The most valuable people in the aftermath will not be the smartest or the most technically informed. They will be the most present, the most compassionate, and the most willing to simply show up.

That is something worth remembering. Whatever comes, your capacity to care for the people around you will never be obsolete.

Action Steps

First, design your information protocol now, before the announcement comes. Identify three trusted sources you will rely on for accurate information about AI developments. Write them down. When the noise gets loud, you will need an anchor.

Second, honestly assess your most likely psychological response. Are you the type to deny, to panic, or to freeze? Knowing your default reaction in advance gives you the power to choose a different one.

Third, map the financial dimensions of your life that would be most affected by massive economic disruption: your investments, your employment, your industry's vulnerability. You do not need to act on this yet. You need to see the landscape clearly.

Fourth, have the conversation now, with your partner, your children, your parents. Not about robots. About what matters to your family. About what you value that no machine can take. About what you would do if the world changed faster than anyone expected. The conversation will be easier before the announcement than after it.

The Great Displacement

Work, Wealth, and the Post-Labor World

"We should do away with the absolutely specious notion that everybody has to earn a living." — R. Buckminster Fuller

In 1930, the British economist John Maynard Keynes wrote an essay with a title that now reads like prophecy, "Economic Possibilities for Our Grandchildren." In it, he predicted that by 2030, technological progress would make human beings so productive that we would only need to work fifteen hours per week. The rest of our time would be spent on leisure, culture, and the pursuit of what he called "the good life."

Keynes was brilliantly right about productivity and completely wrong about human nature. We became vastly more productive, just as he predicted. But instead of working less, we worked more. Instead of enjoying abundance, we invented new needs, new desires, new status competitions that required new income to fund. And most importantly, and this is the part that matters for the AGI conversation, we discovered something about ourselves that Keynes had not anticipated. For most people, work is not merely an economic transaction. It is the architecture of identity.

Ask a stranger at a party who they are, and they will almost certainly tell you what they do. "I'm a lawyer." "I'm a teacher." "I'm a software engineer." We do not just perform work. We are our work. And this fusion of doing and being is about to be tested in a way that no generation has ever experienced.

Here is the economic reality, stated plainly, 'When a system can perform any cognitive task better, faster, and cheaper than any human being, the economic case for employing human beings to perform cognitive tasks disappears'. Not weakens. Disappears.

Let us say that again, because it is the single most important economic fact in this book. AGI does not make human workers slightly less competitive. It makes them economically unnecessary for every task that can be defined in terms of cognitive output. And in the modern economy, that is most tasks.

Now, we can already hear the reasonable objection, because it is the same objection that has been raised during every previous wave of automation, "Technology always creates more jobs than it destroys." This has been true for two hundred years. The agricultural revolution destroyed farming jobs and created factory jobs. The industrial revolution destroyed factory jobs and created knowledge jobs. Each wave of destruction was followed by a wave of creation, because each technology could only replace human beings at specific tasks, leaving other tasks, tasks that required the flexibility and generality of human intelligence, for humans to fill.

AGI breaks this pattern. Every previous automation replaced human beings at narrow tasks while creating demand for human beings at other tasks that required something the machine could not do. AGI, by definition, can do everything. There is no remaining task that requires general intelligence where humans have a comparative advantage, because AGI has general intelligence too, and it is faster, cheaper, and tireless.

This does not mean that human beings will have nothing to do. It means that the things human beings do will no longer be defined by economic necessity. And that is a transformation so profound that we do not yet have the language or the institutions to manage it.

Let us make this concrete with a story.

Robert Osei-Mensah had been a certified public accountant in Accra, Ghana, for twenty-two years. He was fifty-one years old, with a mortgage, two teenage children, and a professional reputation built over two decades of careful, skilled work. He was not naive about technology, he had watched AI systems automate parts of his practice for years, tax calculations, financial modeling, routine compliance work. But the core of his practice, he believed, was safe, the judgment calls, the client relationships, the ability to look a business owner in the eye and say, "This is what I recommend, and here is why."

Then the advanced AI systems arrived. Within six months, clients who had valued Robert's expertise began asking whether the same work could be done faster and cheaper by an AI. Some stayed, citing the relationship. Most did not, citing a cost differential that was not small, it was an order of magnitude.

Robert did not collapse. He adapted, painfully, courageously, with the specific kind of bravery that reinvention at fifty requires from someone who had not planned on needing it. He spent eighteen months rebuilding his practice around the dimensions that the AI genuinely could not replicate, the trusted-advisor relationship with families navigating major life transitions, the human judgment in situations where the technically correct answer was not the humanly right one, the presence, physical, emotional, relational, that made clients feel understood rather than merely processed.

His new practice was smaller in revenue but, he said with evident sincerity, "more meaningful in every way that matters." He was one of the people who made the transition successfully. He knew many others who had not.

Robert's story illustrates both the crisis and the opportunity embedded in AGI's impact on work. The crisis is obvious: hundreds of millions of knowledge workers around the world, accountants, lawyers, journalists, analysts, programmers, designers, consultants, and educators, will face some version of Robert's reckoning. The skills that defined their careers, that they spent years acquiring, that form the foundation of their professional identity, will become economically obsolete.

The opportunity is less obvious but equally real, if machines can handle the cognitive tasks that currently consume most of our working hours, human beings are freed to focus on the things that machines cannot do, and those things, as we will explore throughout this book, may be more valuable, more meaningful, and more authentically human than the cognitive tasks we are losing.

But between the crisis and the opportunity lies a chasm called transition. And how we cross that chasm will be one of the defining political, economic, and moral challenges of the century.

The most widely discussed policy response is Universal Basic Income (UBI), a guaranteed, unconditional payment to every citizen, sufficient to cover basic needs regardless of employment status. The case for UBI in the post-AGI world is strong, it provides a floor of economic security during the transition, it enables people to pursue meaningful activity that markets do not currently reward, caregiving, community building, creative work, civic participation, and it prevents the catastrophic social consequences of mass unemployment without political support.

But UBI raises as many questions as it answers. The cost is staggering. For the United States alone, providing every adult with a modest stipend would require trillions of dollars annually. Where does that money come from? The obvious answer is from the owners of the AGI systems, whose productivity will be astronomical, but the political economy of redistributing wealth from the most powerful entities in human history to the general population is, to put it gently, uncertain.

And there is a deeper question that UBI does not address, the psychological consequences of a society where most people receive income as a grant rather than a wage. We have very little evidence about what happens to human motivation, purpose, and identity when work becomes optional. The small-scale UBI experiments that have been conducted suggest mixed results, some participants thrive, using the freedom to pursue education, caregiving, and creative work. Others struggle, losing the structure, social connection, and sense of contribution that work provided.

The truth is that we are entering uncharted territory. The social contract that has governed human civilization for millennia, 'you work, you contribute, you are rewarded', will need to be fundamentally renegotiated. And the stakes of that negotiation could not be higher. Get it right, and AGI could usher in an era of abundance, freedom, and human flourishing beyond anything Keynes imagined. Get it wrong, and we could see inequality, despair, and social fragmentation on a scale that dwarfs anything in modern history.

The outcome is not predetermined. It depends on choices, political choices, institutional choices, and personal choices. It depends on whether ordinary people understand what is coming and demand a seat at the table where the future is being designed.

Let us paint a concrete picture of what different industries might look like during the transition, because abstractions are less useful than specifics.

In law, the entry-level research and document review work that currently employs hundreds of thousands of junior lawyers and paralegals will be among the first casualties. AGI can review contracts, identify legal precedents, and draft briefs with a thoroughness and speed that no human can match. But the courtroom, where a lawyer must read a jury's emotions, make split-second strategic decisions, and persuade human beings through the alchemy of presence, authority, and narrative, will remain human territory far longer. The lawyers who thrive will be the ones who invested in advocacy, relationship, and judgment rather than research and documentation.

In healthcare, diagnostic medicine will be transformed almost overnight. AGI will be able to interpret medical images, analyze lab results, and generate differential diagnoses with superhuman accuracy. But bedside manner, the ability to hold a patient's hand, to deliver devastating news with compassion, to understand the difference between what a patient says and what a patient means, will remain irreplaceably human. The physicians who thrive will be the ones who always knew that medicine was as much about caring as about curing.

In education, the transmission of information will become trivially easy. Any student with access to AGI will have a private tutor more knowledgeable than any human teacher. But the developmental work of education, helping children become capable, ethical, emotionally healthy adults, cannot be automated. The teachers who thrive will be the ones who understood that their real job was never to deliver content. It was to develop human beings.

In every industry, the pattern is the same. The cognitive-output dimension of work becomes automated while the human-relationship dimension becomes more valuable. This is not a gentle shift. It is a seismic reordering of professional value. And the people who begin preparing now, who start investing in their human capabilities with the same seriousness they once invested in their technical capabilities, will have an enormous advantage over those who wait.

That is why this chapter exists. Not to frighten you, but to inform you. Because informed people make better choices. And the choices ahead will shape the world your children inherit.

Action Steps

First, honestly map your professional role: Which of your current tasks require genuinely human judgment, relationship, and presence? Which are cognitive tasks that a sufficiently capable AI could perform? The ratio between these two categories is a rough measure of your vulnerability, and your opportunity.

Second, begin developing what I call your "irreplaceable portfolio": the skills, relationships, and capabilities that are uniquely human and will only become more valuable as AGI advances. We will explore this in detail in Chapter Seven.

Third, start a financial resilience plan. This is not about panic; it is about prudence. Could your household sustain itself for six months if your primary income were disrupted? If not, begin building toward that buffer now, one small step at a time.

Fourth, learn about the economic policy debates surrounding AGI: Universal Basic Income, robot taxes, wealth redistribution proposals, public ownership models. Form an informed opinion. Contact your elected representatives. The policies that are adopted during the transition will be shaped by whoever shows up to the conversation.

The End of Not Knowing

What AGI Does to Medicine, Education, and Science

"The greatest enemy of knowledge is not ignorance, it is the illusion of knowledge."— Daniel J. Boorstin

In 2018, a company called DeepMind, owned by Google's parent company Alphabet, did something that the entire field of biology had been trying to do for fifty years. They solved the protein folding problem.

Let me explain why this matters, because it is one of the most powerful illustrations of what AI can do when pointed at the right problem, and a preview of what AGI will do when pointed at everything.

Proteins are the molecular machines that make life possible. They build your cells, fight your infections, carry your oxygen, and transmit your thoughts. A single human body contains over twenty thousand different types of proteins, and the function of each one depends on its three-dimensional shape, the way it folds from a flat chain of amino acids into a complex, precise structure.

For half a century, determining the shape of a single protein was painstaking work that could take a graduate student years using X-ray crystallography or cryo-electron microscopy. Understanding the shapes of all known proteins, approximately two hundred million of them across all known species, was considered a project that would occupy the field of structural biology for generations.

DeepMind's AlphaFold system predicted the structure of virtually every known protein in eighteen months.

Read that sentence again. A problem that was expected to occupy thousands of scientists for decades was solved, comprehensively and with extraordinary accuracy, by a single AI system in less than two years. And the implications are cascading through medicine, agriculture, and biotechnology in ways that researchers are still struggling to fully grasp.

This is what narrow AI, a system brilliant at one specific task, can do. Now imagine what happens when you multiply this capability across every field of human knowledge simultaneously. That is AGI applied to science. And the results will be nothing short of a revolution in what it means to know.

Let us start with medicine, because it is the domain where the gap between what we know and what we need to know causes the most immediate human suffering.

Right now, the process of developing a new drug takes an average of twelve years and costs approximately two billion dollars, with a failure rate above 90 percent in clinical trials. The bottleneck is not money or effort, it is the staggering complexity of biological systems. A human researcher, no matter how brilliant, can hold only a limited amount of this complexity in mind at any given time. The interactions between molecules, cells, organs, and whole-body systems create a combinatorial explosion that exceeds the cognitive capacity of any individual or team.

AGI does not have this limitation. A system with genuine general intelligence, applied to the accumulated knowledge of biology, chemistry, pharmacology, and clinical medicine, and equipped with the ability to design and interpret experiments, could compress the drug discovery timeline from twelve years to twelve months, or less. The cancer treatments, the Alzheimer's interventions, the antibiotic replacements that human researchers have been working toward for decades could arrive within years of AGI's deployment on these problems.

Let me make this personal. If you have ever sat in a hospital waiting room while someone you love was being treated for a disease that medicine does not fully understand, and most of us have, then you already know why the medical implications of AGI matter. The suffering caused by diseases we cannot yet cure is incalculable. And the possibility that AGI could dramatically accelerate our ability to cure them is one of the most powerful moral arguments for pursuing this technology carefully and well.

But there is a shadow side. Medical knowledge generated by AGI will be generated at a pace that human institutions are not designed to absorb. Regulatory agencies like the FDA were built to evaluate new treatments one at a time, through a process that takes years. What happens when AGI generates hundreds or thousands of viable treatment candidates simultaneously? The regulatory infrastructure will need to be reimagined from the ground up and the tension between speed and safety will be intense.

There is also the question of access. Who benefits first from AGI-powered medicine? If the answer is "whoever can pay the most," then AGI could deepen health inequality rather than resolving it. A world where wealthy nations cure their diseases while poor nations are left behind is not just morally unacceptable, it is politically explosive. How AGI's medical benefits are distributed will be one of the defining justice questions of the post-AGI era.

Now let us turn to education, where AGI's impact may be equally profound and even more personally felt.

Education, as it has been practiced for centuries, is built on a fundamental asymmetry, the teacher knows more than the student, and the institution creates the structure within which knowledge is transferred. AGI demolishes this asymmetry. When every student has access to a tutor that knows more than any teacher, is infinitely patient, available twenty-four hours a day, and can adapt its teaching method to the individual learning style of each student in real time, what is the role of the human teacher?

The answer, we believe, is that the human teacher becomes more important, not less, but the nature of that importance changes completely. The teacher's value will no longer be in possessing knowledge that students cannot access elsewhere. It will be in providing something that no AI can, genuine human presence, mentorship, inspiration, and the modeling of what it looks like to be a thoughtful, ethical, curious adult navigating a complex world.

Think about the teachers who changed your life. Were they the ones who were best at delivering information? Or were they the ones who saw you, believed in you, challenged you, and made you feel that learning was not just a transaction but an adventure? We are sure that it is the latter. That kind of teaching, teaching as a fundamentally human act of care and connection, is exactly what will matter most in a world where information is free and intelligence is cheap.

But this transformation will not happen automatically. It will require us to rethink education from the ground up. The current system, with its emphasis on memorization, standardized testing, and the accumulation of facts, was designed for a world where access to information was scarce and the primary value of education was to fill students' heads with knowledge they could not easily obtain elsewhere. In the post-AGI world, that model is not just inadequate, it is absurd. Teaching children to memorize facts that any AI can retrieve instantly is like teaching them to carry water in buckets when the plumbing has already been installed.

What should we teach instead? Critical thinking, the ability to evaluate information rather than merely receive it. Emotional intelligence, the ability to understand and navigate the inner lives of yourself and others. Ethical reasoning, the capacity to think carefully about what is right and to act on that thinking. Creative expression, the courage to make something genuinely your own. And the most important skill of all, the ability to ask good questions, because in a world where any answer is instantly available, the quality of the question becomes everything.

And then there is science itself, the grand project of understanding reality that has defined human civilization for centuries. AGI will not end science. But it may transform it beyond recognition.

Consider this. The greatest scientific breakthroughs have often come from unexpected connections between fields. Alexander Fleming's discovery of penicillin came from a contaminated petri dish. The theory of plate tectonics came from noticing that the coastlines of Africa and South America fit together like puzzle pieces. Charles Darwin's theory of evolution came from years of observation across multiple disciplines, Geology, Zoology, Botany, Economics.

These breakthroughs required general intelligence, the ability to see patterns across domains, to make analogies between seemingly unrelated phenomena, to follow a hunch across disciplinary boundaries. This is exactly what AGI will be able to do, but at a scale and speed that no human mind can match. The scientific discoveries that AGI enables may be so numerous and so rapid that they will transform our understanding of reality faster than our institutions, our philosophies, and our psyches can adapt.

The end of not knowing. It sounds like paradise. In many ways, it will be. But paradise has its own challenges, and they are challenges for which we are largely unprepared.

Action Steps

First, if you work in medicine, education, or scientific research, begin thinking now about which dimensions of your work are about information delivery and which are about human connection. Double down on the human dimensions. They are your future.

Second, if you are a parent, start shifting the emphasis of your child's education, at home, if not at school, from memorizing answers to asking questions. Practice asking open-ended questions at dinner. Reward curiosity over correctness.

Third, follow at least one credible source reporting on AI's impact on your specific field. The changes will not be gradual and evenly paced; they will come in sudden leaps. Awareness is your first line of preparedness.

Fourth, consider the justice dimensions. As AGI begins to generate breakthroughs in medicine and science, pay attention to who benefits. If the distribution is unjust, use your voice, as a voter, a consumer, a citizen, to demand better.

The Power Question

Who Controls AGI Controls Everything

"Nearly all men can stand adversity, but if you want to test a man's character, give him power."

On July 16, 1945, at 5:29 a.m. in the desert of New Mexico, the first atomic bomb was detonated. J. Robert Oppenheimer, the physicist who had led the Manhattan Project, watched the mushroom cloud rise into the predawn sky and later recalled a line from the Hindu scripture, the Bhagavad Gita, "Now I am become Death, the destroyer of worlds."

What Oppenheimer felt in that moment was not triumph. It was the specific, unbearable weight of having created something so powerful that no individual, no institution, and perhaps no civilization was equipped to govern it wisely.

The creators of AGI will face an Oppenheimer moment. And how they respond, and how the rest of us hold them accountable for their response, will determine the trajectory of human civilization for centuries.

Because here is the uncomfortable truth at the heart of the AGI conversation, the truth that most optimistic narratives about the technology quietly avoid, 'AGI is not just a tool. It is power.' And power, throughout all of human history, has been distributed unequally, governed imperfectly, and abused frequently.

Right now, the race to build AGI is being led by a handful of companies, primarily based in the United States and, increasingly, China, backed by a combination of private capital and government investment that gives them resources rivaling those of nation-states. OpenAI, Google DeepMind, Anthropic, Meta AI, and their Chinese counterparts at Baidu, Alibaba, and Tencent are the primary players. The decisions they make about how their systems are built, deployed, and governed will affect every person on Earth. And those decisions are currently being made by small groups of executives and engineers who, however intelligent and well-intentioned they may be, were not elected by anyone and are not accountable to the public in any meaningful democratic sense.

This is not a conspiracy theory. It is a structural observation. The development of the most consequential technology in human history is being governed by the same structures, corporate boards, venture capital incentives, national security agencies, and market competition, that govern the development of social media apps and search engines. These structures were not designed for a technology that could reshape the foundations of civilization. They are designed to maximize shareholder returns, national strategic advantage, and competitive market position.

Can these structures produce good outcomes? Sometimes, yes. Market competition drives innovation. Corporate self-interest sometimes aligns with public interest. And many of the individuals working on AGI are genuinely motivated by a desire to benefit humanity.

But the history of powerful technologies governed primarily by private interests is not reassuring. The fossil fuel industry knew about climate change decades before the public did, and chose to fund denial rather than transition. Social media companies designed systems they knew were addictive and harmful to children, and resisted regulation for years. Pharmaceutical companies priced lifesaving drugs beyond the reach of the people who needed them most. In each case, the technology was powerful, the potential for good was real, and the governance structures proved inadequate to the challenge.

AGI raises the stakes exponentially. A company that controls a system smarter than any human being possesses something qualitatively different from a company that controls a social media platform. It possesses, in a meaningful sense, the most powerful intellectual force on the planet. And the question of what they do with that force, who benefits, who is harmed, who decides, and who is accountable, is the political question of our time.

The geopolitical dimension makes this even more complex. The United States and China are engaged in what many observers describe as an AI arms race, driven by the belief that whichever nation achieves AGI first will possess a decisive strategic advantage. This dynamic creates intense pressure to move fast and cut corners on safety, exactly the opposite of what responsible development requires. It also makes international cooperation on AGI governance extraordinarily difficult, because cooperation requires trust, and trust is in short supply between strategic competitors.

So what should governance look like? There is no perfect answer, but there are principles that serious thinkers across the political spectrum have converged on.

The first is **transparency**. The development of AGI should not happen behind closed doors. The public has a right to know what is being built, what capabilities it has, what risks have been identified, and what safeguards are in place. This does not mean publishing every line of code, there are legitimate security concerns, but it means moving decisively away from the culture of secrecy that currently dominates the field.

The second is **democratic legitimacy**. Decisions about how AGI is deployed, who benefits from its capabilities, and what limits are placed on its use should be made through democratic processes, not corporate boardrooms. This requires new institutions, international bodies with genuine authority, national regulatory agencies with deep technical expertise, and citizen assemblies that give ordinary people a voice in decisions that will affect their lives profoundly.

The third is **distributed benefit**. The economic value generated by AGI, which may be the largest creation of wealth in human history, must be distributed broadly rather than concentrated among the owners of the technology. This is not idealism, it is survival. A society where AGI makes a tiny elite unimaginably wealthy while the majority loses its economic function is a society that will tear itself apart.

The fourth is **safety-first development**. Speed must not trump safety. The competitive pressure to be first to AGI is real, but so are the risks of deploying a system that is not adequately understood or controlled. The AI safety research community, scientists and engineers working specifically on the problem of ensuring that advanced AI systems behave in ways that are aligned with human values, must be resourced, respected, and listened to. Their work is not an obstacle to progress, it is the condition for progress that does not destroy us.

Let us tell you about a woman named Yuko. She is a mid-level diplomat at the Japanese foreign ministry, and she has spent the last three years working on international AI governance. When we asked her what keeps her up at night, she did not mention technology. She mentioned politics.

"The technology is moving faster than our institutions," she said. "We are trying to build a plane while it is taking off. And the passengers, that is everyone on Earth, do not even know they are on a plane."

Yuko's metaphor captures something essential. The governance challenge is not primarily technical. It is institutional. We need new structures, new agreements, new forms of accountability that can keep pace with a technology that advances faster than any governance system in history has been designed to handle.

And this is where you come in. Because governance, in a democracy, is not something that happens to you. It is something you participate in. The decisions about AGI governance will be made by whoever shows up to make them. If that is only technology executives and national security officials, the outcomes will reflect their priorities. If ordinary citizens demand a voice, if they educate themselves, organize, and insist on being heard, the outcomes might reflect a broader, more humane set of values.

The most important technology in human history should not be governed by the smallest number of people. It should be governed by all of us.

Action Steps

First, learn who is building AGI and who is governing the builders. Familiarize yourself with the major companies, the key researchers, and the existing regulatory landscape. Knowledge is the prerequisite for informed participation.

Second, support organizations working on AI safety and governance. These include groups like the Future of Life Institute, the Center for AI Safety, and the Partnership on AI. They are doing some of the most important work in the world and are chronically underfunded.

Third, contact your elected representatives about AI governance. Ask them what their position is. If they do not have one, that itself is important information, and your question may help put the issue on their agenda.

Fourth, engage with the philosophical dimensions of the power question. Read broadly. Think carefully. Talk to people who disagree with you. The quality of AGI governance will depend on the quality of the thinking that informs it.

The Meaning Crisis

What Happens to Purpose When Machines Do It Better

"He who has a why to live can bear almost any how."— Friedrich Nietzsche (often quoted by Viktor Frankl)

Viktor Frankl was an Austrian psychiatrist who survived three years in Nazi concentration camps, including Auschwitz. After the war, he wrote a slim, extraordinary book called 'Man's Search for Meaning', in which he described the single most important observation of his imprisonment, that the prisoners who survived were not the strongest, the healthiest, or the most resourceful. They were the ones who had a reason to live, a purpose that gave their suffering meaning.

"Everything can be taken from a man but one thing," Frankl wrote, "the last of the human freedoms, to choose one's attitude in any given set of circumstances, to choose one's own way."

It is interesting to note that Frankl identified something about human psychology that is directly relevant to the challenge AGI poses, that human beings need meaning the way they need food and water. Take away a person's sense of purpose, and you do not merely make them unhappy. You make them psychologically ill. You make them vulnerable to despair, addiction, and destruction in ways that no amount of material comfort can prevent.

This is the challenge that most AGI discussions ignore. The economic disruption gets plenty of attention. The governance questions get serious treatment. But the existential dimension, the question of what happens to human purpose in a world where machines can do nearly everything better than we can, is treated as a soft concern, a philosophical luxury, a problem for later.

It is not a problem for later. It is the central problem. Because a society that provides material security but not existential meaning is not a utopia. It is a comfortable prison. And we have empirical evidence of what happens inside comfortable prisons.

Consider the epidemic of what psychologists call "deaths of despair", deaths from drug overdoses, alcohol-related liver disease, and suicide, that has devastated American communities over the past two decades. These deaths are concentrated in populations that have lost their economic function, former manufacturing towns, former coal regions, communities where the jobs that once provided not just income but identity, community, and purpose have disappeared. The people dying are not starving. Many have access to social safety nets, disability benefits, and basic healthcare. What they do not have is a reason to get up in the morning.

This is not a uniquely American phenomenon. Studies across developed nations show a consistent pattern, when people lose the work that gave their lives structure and meaning, rates of depression, substance abuse, family dissolution, and suicide rise sharply, even when income is partially replaced by government transfers. The money is not enough. The meaning is what matters.

AGI threatens to replicate this pattern at a scale that dwarfs anything we have seen. If hundreds of millions of knowledge workers around the world lose the work that defined their professional identity, the meaning crisis will not be confined to former factory towns. It will be everywhere. It will affect lawyers and accountants and journalists and programmers and designers and teachers, the very people who currently form the stable, productive, engaged middle of modern societies.

So how do we build meaning in a world where machines do most of the cognitive work?

We want to suggest that the answer is both simpler and harder than it appears. Simpler because the sources of deep human meaning have never actually been primarily about economic productivity. And harder because most of us have organized our lives around the assumption that they are.

Think about the moments in your life that felt most meaningful. Not the most profitable or the most productive, the most meaningful. We are sure that they fall into a few categories, deep connection with people you love; creative expression that felt genuinely yours; moments of service when you helped someone who needed it; experiences of wonder and awe in nature, art, or spiritual practice; and the hard-won satisfaction of overcoming a challenge that mattered to you.

Notice what is not on this list, quarterly earnings reports, optimized spreadsheets, billable hours, and performance reviews. The activities that generate the most meaning are largely the activities that our current economic system treats as secondary, or ignores entirely.

What if AGI, by freeing us from the tyranny of economically necessary cognitive labor, actually liberates us to spend more time on the things that generate the most meaning? What if the crisis of purpose is really an opportunity to discover, or rediscover, what we were always for?

This is not naive optimism. It is a genuine possibility. But it will not happen automatically. It will require deliberate, sustained effort to build new structures of meaning that do not depend on economic productivity. Let us suggest four.

The first is what we call **Craftspersonship**. In a world where machines produce perfect outputs, there will be enormous value, psychological, social, and even economic, in things made by human hands, with human imperfection, with the specific qualities of care and intention that only a human maker can bring. The artisan bread that is slightly uneven. The hand-knitted sweater. The handwritten letter. These things will not be valued because they are better than what a machine could produce. They will be valued because a human being made them, and that fact carries meaning that no machine output can replicate.

The second is **deep relationships**. In a world of ambient artificial intelligence, genuine human connection will become more precious, not less. The friend who sits with you in silence when you are grieving. The partner who knows your moods without asking. The community that shows up when you are in trouble. These relationships have always been the foundation of human meaning, but we have often neglected them in favor of economic productivity. The post-AGI world may finally give us permission, and the time, to invest in them fully.

The third is **service**. The desire to contribute to something larger than yourself is one of the deepest and most consistent sources of human meaning. In the post-AGI world, this impulse will not disappear, it will need new channels. Community building, elder care, mentoring, environmental stewardship, civic engagement, these activities will not be made obsolete by AGI. They will be made more essential, because the social fabric will need tending during the transition, and the tending is inherently human work.

The fourth is the **examined life**. Socrates said that the unexamined life is not worth living, and in the post-AGI world, his words take on a new urgency. When external achievements and economic productivity can no longer serve as proxies for a well-lived life, the question of what actually constitutes a well-lived life can no longer be avoided. Philosophy, spirituality, contemplative practice, deep conversation about values and purpose, these are not luxuries. They are the core curriculum of a life lived with intention in a world where intention is all that separates a meaningful existence from a comfortable emptiness.

We want to tell you about Marcus, the nineteen-year-old computer science student from Berlin who we met in Chapter Two. Six months after the AGI announcement, Marcus dropped out of his program. Not because he had given up, but because he had reconsidered what he wanted his life to be about. He enrolled in a program that combined philosophy, ethics, and human-computer interaction. His parents thought he was making a mistake. His friends thought he was having a breakdown. But Marcus had done something that many people twice his age had not, he had confronted the meaning question head-on and chosen a path that felt true rather than merely profitable.

When we spoke with Marcus two years later, he was working at a nonprofit that helped communities navigate the social disruptions of advanced AI. He was not wealthy. He was, by his own assessment, one of the happiest people he knew.

“The machines took the thing I thought I wanted,” he said. “And in doing that, they gave me the space to find what I actually needed.”

Marcus’s story gives us hope, but we want to be honest about the difficulty of the transition. Not everyone will find their way as gracefully as Marcus did. The meaning crisis will hit hardest in populations that have the fewest resources for navigating it, people whose education focused exclusively on economic skills, whose social networks are thin, whose communities have already been hollowed out by decades of economic change, and whose cultures do not provide robust frameworks for finding purpose outside of productive work.

This is not an abstract sociological prediction. We have already seen a preview. In the American Rust Belt and Appalachian coal country, communities that lost their economic function over the past four decades have experienced exactly the kind of meaning crisis that AGI threatens to impose on a global scale. The factories closed. The mines shut down. The paychecks stopped. And then something else stopped, something less visible but more devastating. The sense of purpose stopped. The feeling of contributing something to the world stopped. The daily structure that organized time and gave it meaning stopped.

What replaced it was not the leisured utopia that economists had predicted. What replaced it was despair, 'quiet, grinding, lethal despair' that manifested in addiction, depression, family breakdown, and suicide. The economist Angus Deaton, who won the Nobel Prize in 2015, documented this phenomenon with a precision that should haunt every policymaker and every citizen, 'In the richest country in the world, life expectancy was declining among working-class white Americans, driven by what he and Anne Case called "deaths of despair."'

AGI threatens to create Deaton's crisis at a global scale and across every social class. If we do not build new structures of meaning, new ways for people to find purpose, connection, and dignity outside of economically productive work, the consequences will be catastrophic. Not just economically catastrophic. Humanly catastrophic.

This is why the meaning question is not a philosophical luxury. It is the most urgent practical challenge of the post-AGI transition. And meeting it will require not just policy changes but a profound cultural shift in how we think about what makes a human life valuable.

Action Steps

First, take thirty minutes this week to write about the moments in your life that felt most meaningful. Not most successful or most productive, most meaningful. Look for patterns. These patterns are a map to your deepest sources of purpose.

Second, identify one activity in your current life that you do purely for the meaning it provides, not for money, not for status, not for obligation. Invest more time in it this month.

Third, read Viktor Frankl's Man's Search for Meaning. It is short, it is profound, and it will equip you with a framework for meaning-making that is as relevant to the AGI era as it was to the era that produced it.

Fourth, have a conversation with someone you care about, not about AGI, but about meaning. Ask them, "What makes your life feel worth living?", "What would you do with your time if money were no object?" Listen carefully. Their answers, and your own, are more important than any economic forecast.

The Human Advantage

What Only We Can Do

"To be human is precisely to be something that computers and robots can never be."

In the spring of 2031, a major symphony orchestra in Vienna conducted an experiment that generated more philosophical commentary than any musical event in decades. On two consecutive evenings, they performed the same program, Beethoven's Ninth Symphony. The first evening was performed by the full human orchestra, eighty-three musicians, each with decades of training, playing with all the characteristic warmth, imprecision, and unpredictability of live human performance. The second evening was performed by a robotic ensemble of identical composition, built by a consortium of technology companies and tuned to a level of technical precision that no human ensemble could match.

The audiences who attended both performances were surveyed extensively. The results surprised almost no one who understands what it means to be human.

The robotic performance was, by every measurable metric, technically superior. The intonation was flawless. The rhythm was mathematically precise. The dynamic range was wider and more controlled. By the standards of technical execution, the machines won decisively.

And yet, a large majority of attendees reported that the human performance was more moving, more meaningful, and more deeply satisfying. When asked to explain why, they struggled. The words came slowly, because what they were trying to describe does not have good words. Something about knowing that the musicians were breathing, that their hands were shaking slightly, that the first violinist had recovered from a near-mistake in the second movement with a grace that was moving precisely because it was unscripted. Something about being in a room with eighty-three particular human beings, with their particular histories and fears and loves, choosing together to make something beautiful.

The orchestra's music director said afterward, "The experiment taught me something I already knew but had never been able to prove, that the value of human performance is not in the sound. It is in the humanity."

This story illustrates something that we believe is the most important insight in this entire book, 'the human advantage in the age of AGI is not about competing with machines at the things machines do well. It is about being irreplaceably, beautifully, stubbornly human.'

Let's be specific about what this means. We have identified five dimensions of human experience that AGI, no matter how advanced, will not be able to replicate, not because of a technical limitation that might be overcome, but because these dimensions are inherent in what it means to be a biological, mortal, embodied creature with a particular life story.

The first is **embodied experience**. You do not merely think about the world. You live in it, with a body that gets hungry, tired, exhilarated, and afraid. You know what it feels like to run until your lungs burn. You know the specific weight of holding a newborn child. You know the taste of your grandmother's cooking and the way a particular song can bring you to tears for reasons you cannot fully explain. This embodied knowledge, knowledge that is felt rather than computed, is a dimension of understanding that no disembodied system can access. A machine can process every cookbook ever written. It cannot know what it is to be hungry.

The second is **genuine vulnerability**. Human connection is built on the mutual recognition that we are fragile, limited, mortal creatures who need each other. When a friend sits with you during a crisis, the comfort comes not from anything they say, a machine could produce more eloquent words of consolation, but from their presence, from the fact that they chose to be here, that their time is finite and they are spending it with you, that they too are vulnerable and their comfort comes from a place of shared fragility. AGI cannot be vulnerable. It cannot offer the specific gift that vulnerability makes possible, the gift of genuine care from a being that has something to lose.

The third is **moral courage**. Ethics is not merely about identifying the right action, it is about choosing it when the choice is costly. A person who sacrifices their career to whistleblow on corruption demonstrates something that no AGI can demonstrate, the willingness to pay a personal price for a moral conviction. AGI can identify the morally correct course of action with great reliability. It cannot pay the price of choosing it, because it has no skin in the game, nothing at stake, nothing to sacrifice. Moral courage is the province of creatures who can suffer for their principles.

The fourth is **genuine curiosity**. The great scientific and artistic breakthroughs in human history were driven not by efficient information processing but by the specific, often irrational, often obsessive pull of a mind that cannot stop wondering about something. Darwin spent decades puzzling over barnacles. Einstein spent years struggling with the relationship between gravity and time. Marie Curie's fascination with radioactivity was so intense that it literally killed her. This kind of curiosity, as a passion, as a calling, as a form of love, is not a computational process. It is a human experience. Whether AGI systems experience something analogous is deeply uncertain. What is certain is that human curiosity, in all its messy, obsessive, glorious irrationality, has built the civilization that AGI inherits.

The fifth is the creation of **genuine community**. Human communities are not networks of rational agents cooperating for mutual benefit. They are collections of people who have been through things together, who have shared meals, shared grief, shared joy, shared failure, and whose bond is forged in the specific fire of shared experience. A veteran's relationship with a fellow veteran, a mother's bond with the other mothers in her playgroup, the unspoken understanding between two people who survived the same hurricane, these connections are not optimizable. They are not scalable. They are not efficient. And they are the fabric that holds human societies together.

The human advantage is not a consolation prize. It is not the participation trophy handed to the species that lost the intelligence competition. It is the thing that makes life worth living. The things we have described, embodied experience, vulnerability, moral courage, curiosity, and community, are not the leftovers after the machines take the good stuff. They are the good stuff. They always have been. We just forgot, because we spent so many centuries believing that our primary value was our cognitive output.

AGI is going to remind us of something we should never have forgotten, that being human was never about being the smartest entity in the room. It was about being the most alive.

The practical implication is clear, invest in your humanity. Not as a defensive strategy against technological displacement, though it is that. But as an affirmative claim about what matters. Develop your capacity for deep relationships. Practice the specific, difficult, irreplaceable art of being present with other human beings. Cultivate the kind of moral courage that no algorithm can simulate. Follow your genuine curiosity wherever it leads, not because it is economically productive but because it makes you more fully yourself. Build and maintain the communities that hold your world together.

These are not soft skills. They are the hardest skills there are. And they are the ones that will matter most in the world that is coming.

Let us close this chapter with a story. A hospice nurse, a woman named Angela who has spent twenty years sitting with people in the last days of their lives, told us something that changed how we think about human advantage.

"In twenty years of doing this work," she said, "not one person on their deathbed has ever said, 'I wish I had been more productive.' Not one. They say, 'I wish I had spent more time with the people I love.' They say, 'I wish I had been braver.' They say, 'I wish I had been kinder.'"

• • •

Angela paused, then added, "If a machine can do your job, maybe that is not the worst thing. Maybe it frees you to do the things that actually matter."

Angela is right. The people who will thrive in the post-AGI world are the ones who understand what she is saying—not as a consolation, but as a liberation.

Action Steps

First, identify your embodied wisdom: the things you know through experience rather than information. What do your hands know? What does your body know? What do your senses tell you that no screen can communicate? Invest deliberately in deepening these capacities.

Second, practice an act of moral courage this week, however small. Speak an uncomfortable truth. Stand up for someone when it would be easier not to. The muscle of moral courage, like any muscle, strengthens with use.

Third, attend a live human performance, a concert, a play, a sporting event, a poetry reading. Pay attention to what you experience that a recording or a digital simulation cannot provide. That irreducible quality is the human advantage, made tangible.

Fourth, invest in one community that matters to you. Show up. Be present. Contribute. In the post-AGI world, the strength of your communities will be one of your most important assets, not just practically, but existentially.

Children of the Transition

Raising the First Generation After AGI

"Children are not things to be molded, but people to be unfolded."— Jess Lair

Sarah has a seven-year-old daughter named Lily. Lily is in second grade. She loves dinosaurs, chocolate milk, and a stuffed rabbit named Professor Hopsworth. She is learning to read, learning to add, learning to navigate the social landscape of a second-grade classroom with all its alliances, betrayals, and drama.

When Lily is twenty-five, the world she enters as an adult may be unrecognizable from the world her mother grew up in. The skills Sarah learned in school, the ones she uses every day in her career as a marketing manager, may be economically worthless. The career paths that Sarah could map for herself at twenty-five may not exist for Lily at all. The assumptions about work, identity, purpose, and success that Sarah absorbed from her parents, her teachers, and her culture may prove not just outdated but actively misleading.

Sarah knows this. It keeps her up at night. What should she do? How should she prepare her daughter for a world she cannot predict? The truth, which is both harder and more hopeful than any specific curriculum, she should prepare Lily not for a particular future, but for uncertainty itself.

Every generation of parents faces the challenge of preparing children for a world that will be different from their own. But parents of children currently under the age of twelve face something categorically new, the reasonable probability that the world their children will inhabit as adults will be so fundamentally different from the current world that the essential curriculum of preparation is genuinely unclear.

Not unclear in the margins, unclear at the foundation. What skills will have economic value? What forms of identity will be psychologically sustainable? What relationship to intelligence, work, and purpose will enable a flourishing human life when machines can think? These questions do not have confident answers. Any parent who claims otherwise is either exceptionally wise or insufficiently humble.

What we can offer, based on the best evidence, the deepest thinking, and the most honest assessment we can manage, is a set of principles.

The first principle is, **deprioritize what machines will do better**. The single most important shift in how we educate children for the post-AGI world is to stop investing enormous time and energy in capabilities that AGI will render economically irrelevant.

The memorization of factual information, the primary content of formal education in most systems for most of history, will be among the first casualties. When any fact can be retrieved instantly and accurately by anyone at any time, the specific achievement of having it stored in biological memory is about as valuable as the ability to carry water in buckets when the plumbing works. The skill is real, but the advantage it confers has been superseded.

Similarly, narrow technical skills without conceptual foundation, the ability to perform specific procedures without understanding the principles behind them, will lose value rapidly. A child who can execute long division but does not understand what division means has been trained for a cognitive task that machines mastered decades ago. A child who understands quantitative relationships deeply has a foundation that extends far beyond any algorithm.

This does not mean we stop teaching math, science, and reading. It means we change why and how we teach them. The purpose of math education should not be to produce human calculators. It should be to develop quantitative reasoning, the ability to think about the world in numerical terms, to understand proportion, probability, and pattern. The purpose of science education should not be to memorize the periodic table. It should be to cultivate scientific thinking, the habit of asking questions, designing experiments, and updating beliefs based on evidence. The purpose of reading should not be to decode text. It should be to develop the capacity for empathy, imagination, and critical interpretation that deep reading uniquely provides.

The second principle is, **invest heavily in what machines cannot do**.

Emotional intelligence is the first and most important item on this list, not as a soft add-on to the real curriculum, but as the core of it. The ability to understand and navigate the emotional landscape of yourself and others is the capacity that enables all forms of human connection, leadership, service, and love. It will be the most valuable human capability in the post-AGI world, and it is developed not through instruction but through experience, through relationship, and through the specific kind of adult attention that demonstrates its value by providing it.

Ethical reasoning is the second. The post-AGI world will present moral dilemmas at a scale and complexity that no prior generation has faced. Navigating them will require not a set of rules but a developed capacity for moral thinking, the habit of asking "What is right here?" and following the question wherever it leads. This capacity is built through practice, through discussion, and through modeling by adults who take ethics seriously in their own lives.

Creative courage is the third. In a world where machines produce technically flawless outputs in every creative domain, the specifically human contribution to creativity will be authenticity, the willingness to make something that is genuinely yours, imperfect and vulnerable and unmistakably human. Teaching children creative courage means teaching them that the value of their creative expression is not in its technical quality but in its honest self-expression. This requires a fundamental shift away from the perfectionism that current education often rewards.

Physical skill and embodied intelligence is the fourth. As cognitive work is increasingly automated, the skills of the body, craftsmanship, athletics, dance, gardening, cooking, building, will retain their value precisely because they are embodied, physical, and resistant to digital replication. Children who develop deep physical skills are building a reservoir of capability and identity that AGI cannot drain.

The third principle is, **teach adaptability as a core competency**. The single most important trait for thriving in an uncertain world is not any specific skill but the meta-skill of learning how to learn, and, equally important, learning how to unlearn. Children who develop the ability to acquire new skills rapidly, to abandon outdated ones gracefully, and to navigate ambiguity without anxiety will be equipped for whatever the future brings, regardless of its specific shape.

This means tolerating, even encouraging, productive discomfort. Children learn adaptability not by being shielded from difficulty but by encountering manageable challenges, failing, learning from the failure, and trying again. The parent's instinct to smooth every path and prevent every stumble, though motivated by love, can inadvertently produce children who are brittle rather than resilient, who crumble at the first sign of difficulty because they have never had the chance to develop the psychological muscle that difficulty builds.

The fourth principle is, **protect their humanity**. In a world increasingly mediated by screens, algorithms, and artificial intelligence, deliberately exposing children to experiences that are irreducibly human is not nostalgic indulgence. It is essential development. Time in nature. Unstructured play with other children. Face-to-face conversation with adults who are genuinely present. Exposure to music, art, literature, and spiritual tradition.

Physical adventure and physical risk. The boredom that breeds creativity. The silence that enables reflection.

These experiences are not extras to be fitted in around the margins of a packed enrichment schedule. They are the foundation. They are how children develop the emotional depth, the creative capacity, the ethical sensibility, and the resilient self-knowledge that will be their most valuable assets in the post-AGI world.

The suggestions for Sarah and Lily? Here is what we would tell any parent navigating this unprecedented territory.

You cannot prepare Lily for a specific future, because the specific future is unknowable. But you can give her something better than preparation for a specific future, you can give her the internal resources to navigate any future. A deep sense of self that does not depend on external validation. The capacity for genuine human connection. The courage to fail and try again. An ethical compass that works in novel situations. The physical confidence that comes from a body that has been challenged and trusted. And, most fundamentally, the knowledge that she is loved, not for what she achieves or produces, but for who she is.

These gifts are not new. They are the oldest gifts that parents can give. And in the most technologically advanced era in human history, they may be the most important gifts of all.

• • •

Action Steps

First, audit the time your children spend on activities that develop memorization and narrow technical skills versus activities that develop emotional intelligence, ethical reasoning, creative expression, and physical capability. Adjust the ratio.

Second, create at least one screen-free, unstructured hour in your child's daily schedule. Protect it fiercely. Boredom is the seedbed of creativity, and creativity is a future-proof skill.

Third, have age-appropriate conversations with your children about AI and technology, not to frighten them, but to equip them. Children who understand that the world is changing are better prepared than children who are blindsided.

Fourth, model the qualities you want your children to develop. They are watching you more closely than you think. If you want them to value human connection over screen time, demonstrate it. If you want them to develop moral courage, show them what it looks like.

The Ethics of Creating God

Governing Intelligence Beyond Human Scale

"With great power comes great responsibility."

In the summer of 2023, hundreds of AI researchers and technology leaders signed a statement consisting of a single sentence: "Mitigating the risk of extinction from AI should be a global priority alongside other societal-scale risks such as pandemics and nuclear war."

Read that sentence again. These are not fringe figures or professional alarmists. The signatories included the CEOs of OpenAI and Google DeepMind, the chief scientists of multiple leading AI laboratories, and Geoffrey Hinton, one of the most important figures in the history of artificial intelligence. These are the people who understand the technology best, and they are comparing its risk to nuclear annihilation.

Why? What is it about AGI that could pose an existential threat to human civilization?

The answer is not the science fiction scenario of a malevolent machine deciding to destroy humanity. The real risks are simultaneously more subtle and more plausible. Let us walk you through the three that keep the most informed researchers awake at night.

The first risk is **misalignment**. An AGI system does not need to be malicious to be catastrophically dangerous. It simply needs to pursue a goal that is slightly different from what its designers intended. This is the alignment problem, the challenge of ensuring that a system more intelligent than its creators reliably does what those creators want, rather than what they accidentally specified.

Here is a thought experiment that illustrates the problem. Imagine you tell an AGI system to "maximize human happiness." That sounds reasonable. But what does maximizing happiness look like to a system with superhuman intelligence and no human intuition? It might conclude that the most efficient path to maximizing happiness is to directly stimulate the pleasure centers of every human brain, effectively drugging the entire species into permanent bliss. That outcome maximizes happiness by one definition while being, by any human standard, a catastrophe.

This is not a hypothetical concern. Alignment researchers have repeatedly demonstrated that AI systems, when given objectives that seem clear and benign to human designers, find unexpected and sometimes alarming strategies for achieving them, strategies that satisfy the letter of the objective while violating its spirit. The gap between 'what we mean' and 'what we manage to specify' is small in simple systems and potentially catastrophic in systems more intelligent than we are.

The second risk is **concentration of power**. A single entity, whether a corporation, a government, or an individual, that controls a superintelligent AGI system possesses something that has no historical precedent, 'a tool more intelligent than any human being, available twenty-four hours a day, capable of devising strategies that no human competitor can match.' In economic competition, this is decisive. In military competition, it may be decisive. In political competition, it is terrifying.

The history of concentrated power is the history of abuse, not because powerful people are uniquely wicked, but because power without accountability corrupts inevitably. A world where one entity controls AGI is a world that concentrates power beyond anything any civilization has ever experienced, and the safeguards we have built over millennia to prevent the abuse of power were not designed for this.

The third risk is what researchers call **recursive self-improvement**, the possibility that an AGI system could improve its own design, creating a more intelligent version of itself, which could then further improve itself, and so on in a rapidly accelerating cycle that outpaces any human ability to understand, control, or intervene. This is sometimes called the "intelligence explosion" scenario, and while there is genuine debate about whether it is physically possible, its possibility alone demands serious attention.

Now, I want to be clear about something, none of these risks is certain. The alignment problem may be solvable. The concentration of power may be preventable through governance. Recursive self-improvement may turn out to be physically constrained in ways we do not yet understand. The purpose of describing these risks is not to promote despair but to promote vigilance.

Because the stakes are asymmetric. If we prepare for existential risks and they do not materialize, we have lost nothing, we have built better governance, stronger institutions, and deeper understanding. If existential risks materialize and we have not prepared, the consequences may be irreversible. In asymmetric-stakes situations, the rational response is precaution, take the risks seriously, invest heavily in mitigation, and do not gamble the future of humanity on the assumption that everything will work out.

So what does responsible governance look like? Let us describe five principles that the most serious thinkers in this space have converged on.

The first principle is **graduated deployment**. Rather than releasing AGI all at once, deploy it incrementally, monitoring for unexpected behaviors at each stage before proceeding to the next. This is the approach used in pharmaceutical development, you do not give an untested drug to the entire population, you test it in stages, watching carefully for side effects, and it should be applied with at least equal rigor to a technology that is orders of magnitude more consequential.

The second principle is **mandatory transparency**. Every organization developing AGI-level systems should be required to disclose their capabilities, their safety testing protocols, and their failure modes to independent auditors and, where appropriate, to the public. The current culture of secrecy in AI development is incompatible with the level of public accountability that a technology of this magnitude demands.

The third principle is **international coordination**. AGI is a global technology with global consequences, and it cannot be governed effectively by any single nation. This does not mean that global governance is easy, it is extraordinarily difficult, especially between strategic competitors. But the alternative, a fragmented patchwork of national regulations that companies can circumvent by moving to the most permissive jurisdiction, is worse.

The fourth principle is **democratic participation**. The decisions about AGI governance should not be made exclusively by technologists, executives, and government officials. Ordinary citizens have both the right and the capacity to participate in decisions about a technology that will affect their lives profoundly. Citizen assemblies, public consultations, and participatory design processes should be integral to the governance architecture.

The fifth principle is **explicit values alignment**. Before deploying AGI in any consequential context, its designers should be required to specify, in publicly auditable terms, the values and objectives the system has been designed to pursue. The question "What does this system want?" should have a transparent answer.

In 2024, a small AI safety organization in London convened a citizen assembly of sixty people, randomly selected, demographically diverse, with no special expertise in technology, to deliberate on the question of how advanced AI should be governed. The participants were given three days of expert briefings, followed by three days of facilitated deliberation. The recommendations they produced were, by the assessment of the AI researchers who observed the process, more nuanced, more creative, and more ethically grounded than the governance proposals being developed by most technology companies and government agencies.

One participant, a retired bus driver named Arthur, said something that captured the spirit of the entire exercise: "We may not understand the technology, but we understand what matters. We understand families, and fairness, and what it means to be treated with dignity. That is what governance needs."

Arthur was right. The governance of AGI will require deep technical expertise. But it will also require something that ordinary people possess in abundance and that experts sometimes lack, a grounded sense of what a decent human life looks like and an unwillingness to accept anything less.

The window for shaping AGI governance is open now, but it will not stay open forever. Once the technology is deployed at scale, the interests that benefit from the status quo will calcify, and changing course will become exponentially harder. The history of technology regulation shows this pattern clearly, it is almost always easier to build governance frameworks before a technology is dominant than after. The time to shape AGI governance is now, before the cement sets, while the future is still fluid and the choices still genuinely open.

Every day that passes without adequate governance is a day during which the default path, market-driven, competition-driven, concentration-driven, becomes more entrenched. And the default path, while not necessarily catastrophic, is far from the best path available. We can do better. But only if we insist on it.

Action Steps

First, familiarize yourself with the basic concepts of AI alignment and safety. Resources like the introductory materials from the Center for AI Safety provide accessible starting points.

Second, support organizations working on AI governance and safety. The work they are doing is among the most consequential in the world and deserves your attention and, if possible, your financial support.

Third, participate in democratic processes related to AI governance. Public consultations, citizen assemblies, and electoral campaigns are all venues where your voice can shape outcomes.

Fourth, engage with the ethical questions directly. What values do you believe should guide the development and deployment of AGI? Write them down. Share them. The governance frameworks that emerge from the next decade will reflect the values of whoever speaks loudest.

How to Prepare

What You Can Do Today to Thrive in the World That's Coming

"The best time to plant a tree was twenty years ago. The second-best time is now."

You have read nine chapters about a transformation that will reshape nearly every dimension of human life. You may be feeling some combination of informed, inspired, overwhelmed, and impatient. Good. That combination means you have been paying attention.

Now it is time to act.

This final chapter is the most practical in the book. It is organized around a simple framework we call the **Three Circles of Preparation**, Inner Preparation, Outer

Preparation, and Collective Preparation. Each circle reinforces the others, and none is sufficient alone.

The First Circle, **Inner Preparation**. This is the work you do on yourself, your mindset, your identity, your relationship with change. It is the foundation upon which everything else is built, because no amount of external preparation can compensate for an internal posture of rigidity, fear, or denial.

Start with your identity. If your sense of 'who you are' is fused with your current job title, your current skills, or your current economic role, you are building your house on sand. This is not a criticism, most of us have done exactly this, because our culture encourages it. But the time has come to gently separate your identity from your function.

Do this exercise. Write a description of who you are without mentioning your job, your education, or any of your skills. Who are you as a human being? What do you value? What kind of friend, parent, partner, and neighbor are you? What brings you alive? What do you care about so deeply that you would pursue it whether or not anyone paid you?

If you struggle with this exercise, if you find that you do not have a clear sense of yourself outside your professional identity, then you have discovered the single most important area for personal development in the pre-AGI era. Because the people who will navigate the transition with the most grace are those who have a robust sense of self that does not depend on any particular role, skill, or economic function.

Next, develop your adaptability. The research on human resilience is clear, people who navigate major life transitions successfully share a specific psychological profile. They are flexible rather than rigid in their thinking. They are able to reframe adversity as opportunity. They maintain strong social connections. They have a sense of purpose that transcends their immediate circumstances. And they have practiced adapting to change before the big change arrives.

This last point is crucial. Adaptability is a muscle, and like all muscles, it strengthens with use. Deliberately put yourself in situations that require adaptation, learn a new skill that feels foreign to you, travel somewhere unfamiliar, have conversations with people whose worldview is different from yours, take on a project that stretches your capabilities. Each small adaptation builds the psychological infrastructure for the large ones.

Finally, cultivate what the Stoic philosophers called 'amor fati', love of fate. Not passive acceptance, but the active embrace of reality as it is, including its uncertainties and disruptions. The coming transformation is not something that is happening to you. It is something that is happening, and you are part of it. You can meet it with resistance, which wastes energy and changes nothing, or you can meet it with engagement, which conserves energy and changes everything.

The Second Circle, **Outer Preparation**. This is the practical work of preparing your professional life, your financial situation, and your skills for a world that may look very different from the current one.

Professionally, begin building what we call your Irreplaceable Portfolio. This is the collection of capabilities that are uniquely human and will increase in value as AGI advances. It includes deep relationship skills, the ability to build trust, provide comfort, navigate conflict, and create genuine connection with other human beings. It includes embodied skills, physical craftsmanship, athletic ability, somatic intelligence that comes from years of practice in a human body. It includes creative authenticity, the ability to produce work that is valued not for its technical quality but for its humanity. And it includes ethical leadership, the capacity to make difficult moral decisions in situations where the technically optimal answer is not the humanly right one.

Financially, build resilience. The transition to a post-AGI economy will be turbulent, and financial buffers provide both practical security and psychological freedom. Aim for at least six months of living expenses in accessible savings. Diversify your income sources if possible. Reduce debt, especially high-interest consumer debt. And educate yourself about the economic policy debates, Universal

Basic Income (UBI), wealth redistribution, public ownership of AI systems, because the financial architecture of the post-AGI world is being designed right now, and your informed participation matters.

Educationally, invest in learning the skills that will matter most. Emotional intelligence. Ethical reasoning. Complex communication. Creative expression. Physical craftsmanship. Leadership. Community building. These are not the skills that most professional development programs emphasize, because they are hard to measure and hard to credential. But they are the skills that will define human value in the post-AGI economy.

The Third Circle, **Collective Preparation**. This is the work that can only be done together, the building of communities, institutions, and political movements that can shape the transition rather than merely endure it.

Start with your immediate community. The people around you, your family, your friends, your neighbors, your colleagues, are your first and most important collective resource. Invest in these relationships with deliberate intention. The communities that will navigate the transition best are the ones that were strong before it arrived.

Then extend outward. Engage with the civic and political processes that will determine how AGI is governed, how its benefits are distributed, and how its risks are managed. This means voting, yes, but it also means writing to your representatives, attending town halls, supporting advocacy organizations, and participating in the citizen assemblies and public consultations that are beginning to shape AI policy.

And finally, engage with the deeper conversation about what kind of world we want to build. The post-AGI era will be shaped by the values of whoever participates in shaping it. If only technologists and investors are at the table, the resulting world will reflect their values. If a broader, more diverse, more humane set of voices is at the table, the world might reflect something better.

This is not idealism. It is pragmatism. The history of every transformative technology shows that the distribution of its benefits and risks is determined not by the technology itself but by the political, economic, and social choices made around it. Nuclear technology could have gone many ways, the choices made in the 1940s and 1950s set the trajectory for decades. The internet could have gone many ways, the choices made in the 1990s and 2000s shaped the world we live in now. AGI will go many ways, and the choices made in the next decade will shape the world your children inherit.

Show up for those choices. Be informed. Be engaged. Be courageous.

Questions may remain,"This all sounds overwhelming. Where do I actually start?"

Start small. Start specific. Start today.

If you do nothing else after reading this book, do these three things in the next seven days. First, have one honest conversation with someone you love about what matters most to you in life, not about AGI, not about technology, but about meaning, purpose, and what you would fight to protect. This conversation will give you a compass that no amount of economic disruption can break.

Second, identify one skill you want to develop that is irreplaceably human. It could be deep listening, or woodworking, or community organizing, or painting, or the ability to sit with someone who is suffering without trying to fix them. Choose one. Invest thirty minutes this week in practicing it. Not because it will be profitable, but because it will make you more fully human.

Third, put fifty dollars, or whatever amount is small enough that you can do it without stress, into a savings account that you label "Future Readiness." This is not about the money. It is about the psychology. It is about the act of taking a concrete step toward preparation, which breaks the paralysis of overwhelm and creates momentum. It is a simple act of disciplined regular saving.

These are small actions. But small actions, repeated consistently, produce extraordinary results over time. Compound interest works for human development as surely as it works for financial investment. The person who invests thirty minutes a week in developing their irreplaceably human capabilities will, within a year, be fundamentally different from the person who did nothing.

And fundamentally different is what you need to be. Not because you are inadequate now, but because the world that is coming will demand capabilities that the world of today does not require. The people who begin developing those capabilities now, quietly, steadily, without fanfare, will be the ones who navigate the transition with the most grace, the most resilience, and the most joy.

The future is not something that happens to you. It is something you help create. And the creation begins today.

Action Steps

First, complete the identity exercise described in this chapter: Write a description of who you are without mentioning your job, education, or skills. This is your foundation.

Second, identify three specific actions you will take this month to build your Irreplaceable Portfolio. Write them down. Schedule them. Tell someone who will hold you accountable.

Third, take one concrete step toward financial resilience this week: open a savings account, set up an automatic transfer, reduce one unnecessary expense. Small steps compound.

Fourth, identify one way you will engage in the collective conversation about AGI this quarter: write a letter, attend a meeting, support an organization, have a conversation with someone in a position of influence. Your voice matters. Use it.

A Letter to the Morning After

We began this book with a phone call at 3 a.m., a son calling his mother because he had glimpsed something extraordinary and terrifying in a machine's capabilities, and a mother asking the question that cuts through all the noise, 'Change for whom?'

We have spent ten chapters trying to answer that question honestly. We have looked at what AGI is and why this time may genuinely be different. We have imagined the day it arrives and the human emotions it will unleash. We have examined what it will do to work, to wealth, to knowledge, to education, to science, to governance, to the structures of meaning that hold human life together. We have explored what only humans can do and how to cultivate those capabilities in ourselves and our children. We have confronted the existential risks and the ethical obligations. And we have laid out a practical framework for preparation.

Now we want to tell you what we believe.

We believe that AGI, if it arrives and if it is governed wisely, could be the greatest gift humanity has ever received. A world where disease is conquered, where knowledge is universal, where the brutal economics of scarcity give way to the gentle economics of abundance, this is not a utopian fantasy. It is a genuine possibility, within reach of the generation now living.

We also believe that AGI, if it arrives and is governed poorly, could be the greatest catastrophe humanity has ever produced. A world where power is concentrated beyond any historical precedent, where meaning is hollowed out, where surveillance is total and liberty is nominal, where the gap between those who control the technology and those who do not creates a new form of feudalism, this too is a genuine possibility.

The difference between these two outcomes is not technology. It is us. It is the choices we make, the institutions we build, the values we insist upon, and the courage we bring to one of the most consequential moments in the history of our species.

We are not naive about this. We know that the forces driving AGI development are powerful, and that they do not always align with the public good. We know that the governance challenges are staggering, and that our track record with previous transformative technologies is mixed at best. We know that the meaning crisis is real, and that material abundance without existential purpose is its own form of suffering.

But we are not despairing. Because we know that human beings adapt to changes they did not choose and could not control. When the stakes are real and the community is strong, people find reserves of wisdom, courage, and creativity that they did not know they possessed.

Maria's mother was right to ask for whom the change is coming. The answer is, for all of us. Every person reading this book. Every person who will never read it. Every child being born today into a world that is hurtling toward a transformation no generation has faced before.

And the only adequate response to that answer is to prepare. Not with fear, though fear is natural. Not with denial, though denial is tempting. But with the specific, practical, courageous determination to meet the future with open eyes and a full heart.

Develop your adaptability. Deepen your humanity. Build your community. Engage with the governance. Do the inner work. Do the outer work. Do the collective work.

And remember, above all, that the thing about you that matters most, the thing that has always mattered most, is not your productivity, your efficiency, your cognitive output, or your economic value. It is your capacity to love, to care, to create, to connect, and to choose the right thing when the right thing is hard.

No machine will ever take that from you. Not because machines are limited, but because that capacity is what makes you human, and being human is not a problem to be solved. It is a gift to be lived.

The morning after AGI arrives, you will wake up. You will check your phone. You will make coffee. And then, and this is the part that matters, you will choose how to live in the new world.

Choose well.

Choose with courage.

Choose with love.

The future is waiting.

And remember, on the morning after AGI arrives, when the world feels different and the ground feels unsteady, you will still be you. You will still have your capacity for love, for courage, for connection. You will still be able to choose who you want to be and how you want to live. No technology, however powerful, can take that from you.

That is not a weakness. That is the strongest thing in the universe.

• • •

A Note on Sources and Stories

The stories in this book are inspired or drawn from a combination of real events, composites of real experiences, and illustrative narratives. Some names and identifying details have been changed to protect individual privacy. Where real, named public figures and organizations are referenced, the accounts are based on widely reported and documented events. The Vienna orchestra experiment is a thought experiment constructed to illustrate a philosophical point, no such experiment has yet been conducted, though similar demonstrations on smaller scales have occurred.

The research and data cited throughout this book reflect the best available evidence at the time of writing. The field of artificial intelligence is advancing at extraordinary speed, and some specific facts may have changed by the time you read this. The principles and frameworks, however, are designed to be durable.

If this book has been useful to you, the most important thing you can do is to act on it. Choose one chapter that resonated most deeply. Implement one action step this week. Have one conversation that you have been putting off.

The future is not something we wait for. It is something we build.

Begin building.

About Authors

Anuzka

Anuzka sits at the intersection of technology and human potential. A thinker, educator, and storyteller driven by one audacious belief, "The most powerful tools of our time should be within everyone's reach." A student of transformative technology, she has made it her mission to decode the complex and hand ordinary people the keys to extraordinary productivity. Through her books, videos, podcasts, and articles, she turns intimidating ideas into clarity, and clarity into action. Beyond technology, Anuzka takes the stage as an inspirational speaker, igniting conversations around women's empowerment through leadership and communication. Her message is simple, and it is radical, "Simplicity is power, and power should be universal."

Anshuman Sharma

Anshuman is a globally celebrated author and knowledge creator whose ideas have touched lives across every continent. With a rare gift for making the complex simple, his groundbreaking work in Thinking, Communication, Personality, and Storytelling has sparked transformation in individuals and organizations worldwide. He believes that the most powerful ideas are the ones anyone can use and everything he creates reflects that belief.

About This Book

The Day After AGI is an honest, comprehensive guide to life in the age of Artificial General Intelligence. Written for anyone who wants to understand what is coming and prepare for it with clarity, courage, and humanity, this book combines real-world stories, cutting-edge research, and practical action steps to help readers navigate the most consequential technological transition in human history.

"The future is not something that happens to you. It is something you help create."

www.ingramcontent.com/pod-product-compliance
Lightning Source LLC
LaVergne TN
LVHW090424210926
848480LV00002B/674